RIPLEY'S Believe It or Not!®

WILD ANIMALS

THE MARINE IGUANAS of Galapagos

A Byron Preiss Book

TOR®

A Tom Doherty Associates Book
New York

The Ripley's 100th Anniversary Series:

Weird Inventions and Discoveries
Odd Places
Strange Coincidences
Wild Animals
Reptiles, Lizards and Prehistoric Beasts (Available in June 1992)
Great and Strange Works of Man (Available in August 1992)

Ripley's Believe It or Not!
Wild Animals

A Tor Book
Published by Tom Doherty Associates, Inc.
175 Fifth Ave.
New York, N.Y. 10010

ISBN: 0-812-51289-8

First Tor edition: March 1992

Printed in the United States of America

0 9 8 7 6 5 4 3

INTRODUCTION

Welcome to the special Centennial Edition of "Ripley's Believe It or Not!," the most famous and best known entertainment feature in the world. 1993 will be the hundredth anniversary of Robert L. Ripley's birth. This centennial series is designed to help celebrate that occasion.

Ripley was one of the most fabulous and interesting personalities of the 20th century. He spent his life traveling the globe in pursuit of the odd, bizarre, and incredible-but-true stories that have filled the "Believe It or Not!" pages for over 70 years. During this period, more than 80 million people in 125 countries have been entertained and amazed by Robert L. Ripley's creation. In addition, millions more have marveled at the incredible oddities on display at the Ripley's museums in America, England, Canada, Australia, and Japan.

Ripley's amazing worldwide industry is a true American success story, for it started humbly with one man and an idea.

In 1918, the twenty-five-year-old Ripley was a hard-working sports cartoonist for the New York Globe newspaper. It happened one day that he was stuck for a cartoon to draw. As his daily deadline approached, he was still staring at a blank sheet on his drawing board when inspiration struck. Ripley dug into his files where he kept notes on all sorts of unusual sports achievements. He quickly sketched nine of the more interesting and bizarre items onto his page, and a legend was born. That first page was titled "Champs and Chumps." Ripley's editor quickly came up with a snappier name, and "Believe It or Not!" became an overnight sensation.

In 1929, Ripley published his very first collection of "Believe It or Not!" in book form. It was an immediate success. A few years later his feature was appearing in over 200 newspapers in the United States and Canada alone. But Ripley was just getting started. With financial backing from his newspaper syndicate, Ripley traveled thousands of miles in the next few years. He visited 198 countries, bringing back oddities, antiques, and amazing stories from each place he stopped. The best of these eventually wound up in his famous syndicated feature. The amazing truth is that Ripley supplied at least one "Believe It or Not!" every day for thirty years!

In 1933, Ripley collected many of his fabulous treasures and put them on exhibition in Chicago. Within a year, his "Odditorium" had hosted almost two and a half million people. They lined up around the block to see the displays of shrunken heads, postage-stamp-size paintings, treasures from the Orient, incredibly intricate matchstick models, and wickedly gleaming instruments of medieval torture.

Soon after Ripley died in 1949, his unique collection of oddities was gathered and displayed in the first permanent "Believe It or Not!" museum in St. Augustine, Florida. And, fittingly, Ripley himself became one of its more amazing items. A full-size replica of the man stood at the door, greeting all visitors and giving them a foretaste of the astonishing objects they would see inside.

Although Robert L. Ripley passed away, his work lives on. The Ripley's organization has ceaselessly provided daily "Believe It or Not!" pages through the decades, always reaching a bit farther for those fantastic (but true) stories that stretch the imagination. And they are still actively seeking more. If you know of any amazing oddity, write it down and send it in to:

Ripley's Believe It or Not!
90 Eglinton Avenue East, Suite 510
Toronto, Canada
M4P 2Y3

There are now over 110,000 "Believe It or Not!" cartoons that have been printed in over 300 categories. These include everything from amazing animals to catastrophes to "Wild Animals," the volume you hold right now. So sit back, get comfortable, and prepare to be astonished, surprised, amazed, and delighted. Believe it or not!

THE KLIP SPRINGER
African Antelope
HAS SUCH SMALL FEET THAT
ITS 4 HOOVES CAN FIT ON A DIME

THE HYDRA, a fresh-water polyp
PROPELS ITSELF ALONG BY
TURNING SOMERSAULTS

THE LIVING SUBMARINE

THE HIPPOPOTAMUS CAN CLOSE ITS NOSTRILS AND EARS AT WILL, AND REMAIN SUBMERGED IN WATER FOR *MORE THAN 10 MINUTES AT A TIME*

THE **ATLANTIC PUFFIN** (Fratercula arctica) ALSO KNOWN AS THE "SEA PARROT," CAN KILL AND CARRY UP TO 20 FISH IN ITS BILL, CAUGHT ONE AT A TIME!

THE **WHALE** AND THE **KANGAROO RAT** ARE THE ONLY MAMMALS IN ALL NATURE THAT HAVE 6 OF THEIR 7 NECK VERTEBRAE FUSED TOGETHER

KOKO

THE "TALKING" GORILLA, TAUGHT 500 WORDS IN SIGN LANGUAGE BY TRAINER PENNY PATTERSON OF THE GORILLA FOUNDATION IN WOODSIDE, CALIF., *CRIED FOR TWO DAYS WHEN SHE WAS TOLD IN SIGN LANGUAGE OF THE DEATH OF HER PET CAT*

THE
CRANE

UP TO 5 FEET IN HEIGHT, IS THE WORLD'S TALLEST FLYING BIRD, REACHING ALTITUDES UP TO 30,000 FEET-- IT MATES FOR LIFE, LIVES AS LONG AS 80 YEARS AND ITS CALL CAN BE HEARD MILES AWAY

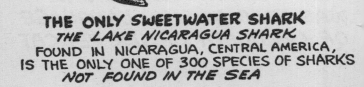

THE ONLY SWEETWATER SHARK
THE LAKE NICARAGUA SHARK
FOUND IN NICARAGUA, CENTRAL AMERICA, IS THE ONLY ONE OF 300 SPECIES OF SHARKS *NOT FOUND IN THE SEA*

A **RARE BIRD** THE GREY LAG GOOSE (Anser anser) LARGEST OF THE WILD GEESE, IS SO FAITHFUL THAT IF ITS MATE DIES IT REMAINS A LONER FOR THE REST OF ITS LIFE-- *AND IT HAS A LIFE SPAN OF 80 YEARS*

THE WATER SHREW

SEEMS TO SHOW AFFECTION
FOR ITS OFFSPRING IN
CAREFULLY COACHING
THEM --*BUT WHEN THEY
ARE DISOBEDIENT
SHE DEVOURS THEM*

POLAR BEARS
CAN SMELL AND
LOCATE PREY
*AT A DISTANCE
OF 20 MILES*

AN ALBINO GIRAFFE
PHOTOGRAPHED IN KENYA
BY COL. SANDY MACNAB,
AN AMERICAN HUNTER
-*AND NEVER SEEN AGAIN*

THE **NEST** OF THE TAILOR-BIRD of India, *IS MADE FROM A SINGLE LEAF.*

IT IS LACED TOGETHER WITH VEGETABLE FIBER BY THE BIRD

THE FEMALE SILVERY-CHEEKED HORNBILL

seals herself in a hollow tree trunk until her chicks are grown. The family is fed by the male 10 to 20 times a day through a chink in the bark!

LANTHANOTUS BORNEANSIS

HALF SNAKE AND HALF LIZARD, WAS BELIEVED EXTINCT FOR 1,000,000 YEARS --*BUT ONE WAS FOUND ALIVE RECENTLY IN SARAWAK, MALAYSIA*

IN A SINGLE NIGHT, A MOLE CAN DIG A TUNNEL OF **223 FT.!**

BALUCHITHERIUM
A HORNLESS RHINOCEROS THAT LIVED 30,000,000 YEARS AGO, CONSIDERED THE LARGEST LAND MAMMAL OF ALL TIME, *STOOD 18 FEET AT THE SHOULDER*

THE
EYEBALLS
OF THE
GIRAFFE
PROTRUDE TO
SUCH AN EXTENT
THAT HE CAN SEE
IN *ALL* DIRECTIONS
WITHOUT TURNING HIS HEAD

THE REAL
"KING KONG"
GIGANTOPITHECUS,
A GIANT APE THAT
LIVED IN THE
EARLY STONE AGE,
WAS NINE FEET
TALL AND WEIGHED
600 LBS.— YET
LATEST SCIENTIFIC
EVIDENCE SUGGESTS
*IT MAY HAVE BEEN
COMPLETELY
WIPED OUT BY
HOMO ERECTUS,
AN ANCESTOR
OF MODERN
MAN*

THE
HIPPOPOTAMUS
LUBRICATES ITS SKIN BY EMITTING FROM SPECIAL
GLANDS A REDDISH FLUID **THAT LOOKS LIKE BLOOD**

ONE PRONG OF THE ANTLERS OF MALE REINDEER

PROTECTS AN EYE FROM DAMAGE IN THEIR FURIOUS BATTLES AT MATING TIME

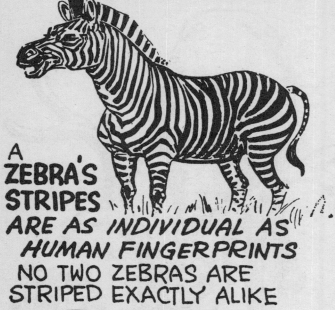

A **ZEBRA'S STRIPES** *ARE AS INDIVIDUAL AS HUMAN FINGERPRINTS* NO TWO ZEBRAS ARE STRIPED EXACTLY ALIKE

FEMALE ELEPHANT SEALS DIVE DEEPER THAN ANY OTHER MARINE MAMMAL AND MAY REMAIN UNDERWATER AS LONG AS 48 MINUTES, SLEEPING PART OF THE TIME AND NOT BREATHING. ON LAND THEY HOLD THEIR BREATH WHILE SLEEPING FOR UP TO 25 MINUTES

A CAT
DOES NOT USE ITS
VOCAL CORDS
TO PURR

WHY DOLPHINS DON'T MIND THE DARK

They locate objects by sonar signal echoes and can recover a dime tossed in the water 40 feet away even when *BLINDFOLDED*

NORTHERN CARIBOU CAN SMELL WITH HIS HIND HOOFS

THE
*AUSTRALIAN
SUGAR
GLIDER*
TO BUILD ITS
NEST BITES OFF
LARGE LEAVES AND
CARRIES THEM TO ITS
HOME SITE *WRAPPED
UP IN ITS TAIL*

A GIANT SWORDFISH MAY WEIGH OVER 1000 POUNDS AND CAN RAM HIS SWORD *THROUGH 6 INCHES OF COPPER-SHEATHED OAK PLANKING*

A COYOTE
HAS SUCH ACUTE HEARING IT CAN PINPOINT THE LOCATION OF A MOUSE MOVING BENEATH *A FOOT OF SNOW*

THE **GLOW** OF THE
FIREFLY FISH
IS PRODUCED BY
A COLONY OF
BACTERIA THAT
DWELL BENEATH
EACH OF ITS EYES

THE QUEEN SCALLOP
ESCAPES FROM PURSUING STARFISH
BY SHOOTING WATER FROM ITS VALVES
-*A FORM OF JET PROPULSION*

THE CARIBOU
IS THE ONLY MAMMAL
THAT WALKS AND RUNS
ON AN EXTRA HOOF
--*WHICH LOOKS LIKE
A LADY'S HIGH HEEL*

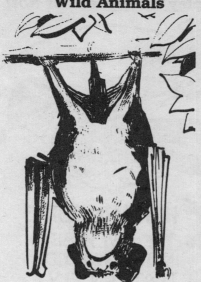

THE **MEXICAN FREE-TAILED BAT** HAS THE FASTEST HEARTBEAT OF ANY MAMMAL - *700 BEATS PER MINUTE*

THE HUMMINGBIRD
IS THE *ONLY* BIRD
IN THE WORLD
THAT CAN FLY
BACKWARDS

THE
BLUE WHALE
WHICH HAS A MOUTH SO
LARGE A FULL-GROWN MAN
COULD STAND INSIDE IT WITH HIS
HANDS RAISED, CAN SWALLOW
NOTHING LARGER THAN A SHRIMP

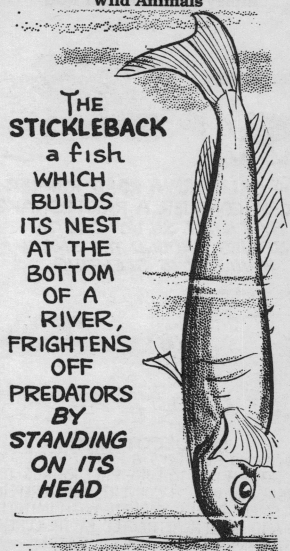

THE **STICKLEBACK** a fish WHICH BUILDS ITS NEST AT THE BOTTOM OF A RIVER, FRIGHTENS OFF PREDATORS *BY STANDING ON ITS HEAD*

THE **CALIFORNIA ROAD RUNNER**
CAN CONQUER A RATTLESNAKE
*BY PILING SHARP CACTUS
SPINES AROUND THE SNAKE
WHILE IT IS SLEEPING*

THE DECOY FISH
(Iracundus signifer) A RARE SPECIES OF
SCORPIONFISH, TO LURE PREY, RAISES ITS
DORSAL FIN WHICH CONVERTS INTO A REPLICA
OF A SMALL FISH COMPLETE WITH IMITATION
EYE AND MOUTH. ATTRACTED BY THE LURE, THE
VICTIM INVESTIGATES AND IS EATEN

THE **WHITE-EARED HONEY EATER** OF AUSTRALIA IS A TIMID BIRD – YET IT STEALS THE HAIR WITH WHICH IT LINES ITS NEST *FROM THE HEAD OF ANY PASSERBY*

THE **WHITE-BACKED VULTURE** of Africa, HAS EYES SO SHARP IT CAN SPOT A PREY *FROM A DISTANCE OF 100 MILES*

THE **SKUNK** PRODUCES ITS MOST OBJECTIONABLE ODOR FROM A CHEMICAL CALLED ETHANETHIOL — WHICH IS SO STRONG THAT ONE TEN-TRILLIONTH OF AN OUNCE CAN BE DETECTED BY THE HUMAN NOSE

THE **BABY PANGOLIN** *IS CARRIED ABOUT ON ITS MOTHER'S TAIL*

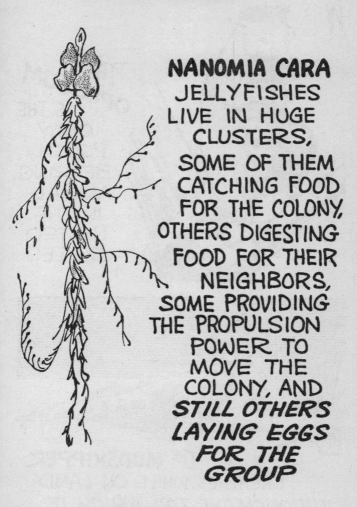

NANOMIA CARA JELLYFISHES LIVE IN HUGE CLUSTERS, SOME OF THEM CATCHING FOOD FOR THE COLONY, OTHERS DIGESTING FOOD FOR THEIR NEIGHBORS, SOME PROVIDING THE PROPULSION POWER TO MOVE THE COLONY, AND *STILL OTHERS LAYING EGGS FOR THE GROUP*

THE **OPOSSUM** IS THE ONLY POUCH-BEARING ANIMAL IN THE UNITED STATES

THE **MUDSKIPPER** BREATHES WHILE ON LAND *THROUGH THE TAIL WHICH IT KEEPS DIPPED IN THE WATER*

THE **CRESTED BELL-BIRD** BEST VENTRILOQUIST IN THE ANIMAL WORLD, FOILS PREDATORS BY *MOVING ITS VOICE FROM TREE TO TREE*

THE KOALA BEAR
OF AUSTRALIA
NEVER DRINKS
THE NAME "KOALA"
MEANS "NO DRINK"

THE **PECTORAL FIN** OF A WHALE IS AMAZINGLY SIMILAR TO A HUMAN ARM WITH A "SHOULDER BLADE," AN "UPPER ARM," AN "ELBOW," A "WRIST" AND 5 "FINGERS"

THE CATFISH
tastes and smells food through its whiskers, tail, fins and skin!

THE **SHARK**
COMES IN OVER 250 SPECIES--
OF WHICH *ONLY SOME 30*
ARE DANGEROUS TO MAN

THE **ARMADILLO**
HAS AS MANY
AS 104 TEETH--
MORE THAN ANY OTHER
LAND MAMMAL

THE KLIPSPRINGER

AN AFRICAN DWARF ANTELOPE,
WEIGHING 30 LBS. AND STANDING
2 FT. HIGH, MARKS ITS TERRITORY
OFF LIMITS TO OTHER ANTELOPES
BY WETTING A TWIG WITH A
SECRETION OBTAINED BY
PRESSING THE TWIG INTO
OPEN GLANDS UNDER ITS EYES

HUGE LAND CRABS in Cuba, CAN OUTRACE A HORSE

THE PORCUPINE
CANNOT "SHOOT" ITS QUILLS
IT DRIVES ITS QUILLS INTO A FOE WITH ITS TAIL

A **ROBIN** CAN HEAR AN EARTHWORM MOVING

THE GLOBE FISH
WHEN SWIMMING TIRES IT,
*FLOATS BY PUFFING
ITSELF UP WITH AIR*

DUCKS AND OTHER BIRDS
CAN WALK ON FREEZING-
COLD SNOW BECAUSE THEIR
FEET HAVE LITTLE BLOOD
AND ARE HARDLY AFFECTED
BY LOW TEMPERATURES

THE ELEPHANT SHREW

NEVER CLOSES ITS EYES

THE **ANGLER FISH** of Panama
WHICH LURKS AT DEPTHS OF UP TO
7,000 FEET ATTRACTS ITS FOOD BY
A LIGHT ON THE END OF ITS NOSE

THE FEROCITY
OF A MALE BISON
IS INDICATED BY THE
SIZE OF ITS BEARD

THE FARMER'S FRIEND

ONE OWL
CAN CONSUME
10 MICE IN A
SINGLE MEAL
--WHICH CAN
SAVE A FARMER
AS MUCH AS
360 LBS. OF
VEGETATION
A YEAR

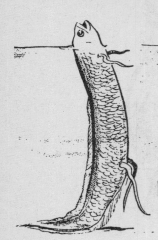

THE
**AMAZON BASIN
LUNGFISH**
MUST STAND ON
ITS TAIL TO
BREATHE ABOVE WATER
--*OR IT WILL
DROWN*

THE **WORLD'S LARGEST RODENT**
THE CAPYBARA OF EASTERN
PANAMA AND SO. AMERICA
GROWS TO A WEIGHT OF
MORE THAN 100 LBS. AND
A LENGTH OF 4 FEET

THE **RED-CAPPED MANGABEY** of Africa, COMMUNICATES WITH OTHER MONKEYS OF THE SAME BREED *BY BLINKING ITS WHITE EYELIDS LIKE SEMAPHORES*

THE ELEPHANT SNOUT
AN AFRICAN FISH
COMMUNICATES WITH
OTHER FISH BY EMITTING
AN ELECTRICAL SIGNAL
--*A PISCATORIAL VERSION
OF THE MORSE CODE*

THE FLOWER MOLE
THE STAR-NOSED MOLE HAS A
SNOUT SURROUNDED BY 22
FLESHY GROWTHS THAT LOOK LIKE
THE PETALS OF A FLOWER

ANIMALS

98% of the 500,000,000 species that have existed on earth since the beginning of time are EXTINCT!

OWLS
FLY IN COMPLETE SILENCE
-- *BECAUSE THEIR FEATHERS ARE TIPPED WITH DOWN*

SIBERIAN BROWN BEARS
EAT ONLY FISH HEADS
--BUT THE WHITE-BREASTED BLACK BEARS OF SIBERIA DISCARD THE HEADS OF FISH AND
EAT ONLY THE BODIES

PRAIRIE DOGS
IDENTIFY EACH
OTHER BY
"KISSING."
*EACH PRESSES ITS
TEETH AGAINST THE
OTHER'S FACE*

THE **ROAR OF A TIGER** CAN BE HEARD FOR A DISTANCE OF **2 MILES**

THE **2 EYES OF A LOBSTER—** EACH HAS 13,000 LENSES AND 13,000 INDIVIDUAL NERVE RODS

IF A LOBSTER LOSES AN EYE, IT CAN REGROW ANOTHER— WITH ITS 13,000 LENSES AND 13,000 NERVE RODS

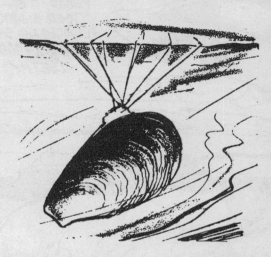

A SUPER-STRONG GLUE

PRODUCED BY MUSSELS ON LONG
THREADS IS SO TOUGH AND
WATER RESISTANT THAT IT
HOLDS THE SHELLS FIRMLY
TO PERCHES POUNDED BY THE
SURF...EVENTUALLY IT MAY BE
USED TO BOND HUMAN BONES
AND SAVE TEETH

IN A 10-YEAR PERIOD, THE TIGER SHARK PRODUCES AND SHEDS OVER 24,000 TEETH!

POLAR BEARS
OFTEN WILL SPEND DAYS ON AN ICE FLOE FLOATING OUT TO SEA--*THEN PLOP INTO THE FRIGID WATER AND SWIM 100 MILES BACK TO SHORE*

THE **SOLENODON** AN INSECT-EATING MAMMAL OF HAITI AND CUBA, TO ESCAPE DETECTION BY A PREDATOR, BURIES ITS HEAD IN THE SAND LIKE AN *OSTRICH*

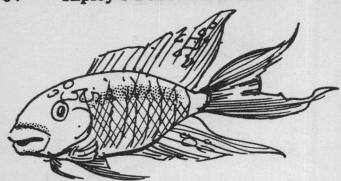

THE PARADISE FISH
of North China,
IN SELECTING HIS MATE
KILLS EVERY PROSPECTIVE BRIDE HE FINDS UNACCEPTABLE

LUCY, a chimpanzee,
USING SIGN LANGUAGE,
ACQUIRED A VOCABULARY OF 80 WORDS

THE GIANT PANDA
EATS 20 TO 40 POUNDS
OF BAMBOO A DAY BUT
HAS A THICK-WALLED
ESOPHAGUS THAT IS
*IMMUNE TO THE
SHARP SPLINTERS*

THE **LARGEST FLYING CREATURE IN HISTORY** THE TEXAS PTEROSAUR, BONES OF WHICH WERE DISCOVERED IN BIG BEND NATIONAL PARK, TEXAS, *HAD A WINGSPAN OF 50 FEET*

CANADIAN BLACK BEARS

WHEN UNSEASONABLE WEATHER IN 1953 PREVENTED THEM FROM HIBERNATING, INVADED PRIVATE HOMES FOR FOOD... AND WHEN SATED EVEN NAPPED ON A VERANDA COUCH

THE **NEST**
OF THE INDIAN
SPARROW IS BOTTLE –
SHAPED, PERCHED
IN THE HIGHEST
AVAILABLE TREE
--AND ILLUMINATED
BY IMPRISONING
FIREFLIES IN
MOIST CLAY

THE **MARINE IGUANAS**
of Galapagos
FIGHT DUELS BY STANDING
FOREHEAD TO FOREHEAD
-AND PUSHING AGAINST
EACH OTHER

THE
RHINOCEROS
HORNBILL
of Asia
and Africa
CAN KILL
A MAN
WITH A
BLOW
OF ITS
BEAK

THE **BOXFISH** IS SO FEROCIOUS THAT WHEN SWALLOWED BY A SHARK, IT CAN BITE ITS WAY TO FREEDOM

THE GOLDEN EAGLE
WILL ATTACK ANYTHING APPROACHING
ITS NEST--*EVEN HELICOPTERS
AND AIRPLANES*

THE **SEA-CUCUMBER,**
A CREATURE OF THE DEEP,
WHEN ATTACKED BY A LOBSTER
OR OTHER PREDATOR, DEFENDS
ITSELF BY EXPELLING ITS OWN
DIGESTIVE SYSTEM--*IN WHICH
THE ATTACKER BECOMES ENTANGLED*
THE SEA CUCUMBER THEN GROWS
ANOTHER DIGESTIVE SYSTEM

THE **COCONUT CRAB**
OF THE INDIAN AND
PACIFIC OCEANS,
WHICH IS **3** FEET
LONG AND WEIGHS
6 POUNDS,
CLIMBS TREES,
HURLS COCONUTS
TO THE GROUND
*AND CAN OPEN
CRACKED ONES
WITH ITS
POWERFUL CLAWS*

THE HOUBARA

WHEN PURSUED BY A HAWK, SPRAYS ITS FOE'S EYES AND FEATHERS WITH A THICK, STICKY FLUID —*BLINDING AND DISABLING IT*

THE THREAD-FINNED FISH

of the Amazon IS THE ONLY FISH THAT LAYS ITS EGGS *OUT OF WATER* — IT LEAPS AND DEPOSITS THE EGGS ON FOLIAGE OVERHANGING THE RIVER

PREHISTORIC HORSES

MILLIONS OF YEARS AGO *WERE ONLY AS TALL AS A RABBIT SITTING ON ITS HAUNCHES*

THE HANUMAN LANGUR

A SLENDER, LONG-TAILED ASIATIC MONKEY, EATS AS ONE OF ITS FAVORITE FOODS A FRUIT CONTAINING THE *DEADLY POISON STRYCHNINE*

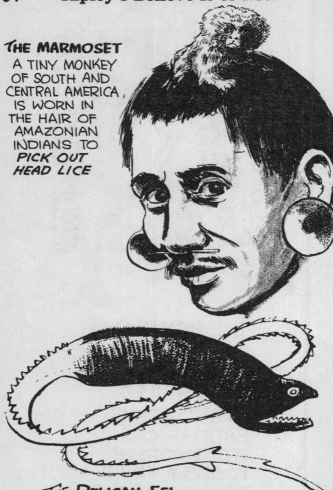

THE MARMOSET
A TINY MONKEY
OF SOUTH AND
CENTRAL AMERICA,
IS WORN IN
THE HAIR OF
AMAZONIAN
INDIANS TO
*PICK OUT
HEAD LICE*

THE PELICAN EEL
WHICH HAS BEEN FOUND AT DEPTHS OF 3,000 FEET,
CAN STRETCH ITS MOUTH AND GULLET
TO SWALLOW FISH LARGER THAN ITSELF

THE
PANGOLIN OF INDIA (Anteater)
WHEN IN DANGER CURLS UP INTO A
BALL AND 3 MEN PULLING AT ITS
TAIL CANNOT UNCURL IT.

THE VAMPIRE BAT
of Mexico and So. America,
DRINKS MORE THAN ITS
WEIGHT IN BLOOD
IN A SINGLE NIGHT

THE **CIVET**
DRIVES OFF ENEMIES WITH A FOUL-
SMELLING SPRAY-- YET THE
LIQUID, CIVET MUSK, IS USED BY
PERFUME MANUFACTURERS

A **PIRANHA**
HAS TEETH SO
SHARP, IT CAN
*RIP OPEN THE
LEATHERY
HIDE OF A
CROCODILE*

THE **SALMON**
NAVIGATES ITS WAY GREAT
DISTANCES TO RETURN TO ITS
NATIVE RIVER TO SPAWN
--*HOMING BY SMELL*

A
SPOTTED HYENA
HAS JAWS SO
POWERFUL IT CAN
*CRUSH THE
LIMBS OF
AN OX*

A SPARROW HAS 14 VERTEBRAE IN ITS NECK --*TWICE AS MANY AS A GIRAFFE*

OWLS HAVE NIGHT VISION *100 TIMES BETTER THAN HUMANS*

A FEMALE RABBIT
is the only animal that in one year can reproduce *10 TIMES ITS OWN WEIGHT*

THE
TAILLESS TENREC
of Madagascar
REGULARLY PRODUCES
THE LARGEST
LITTERS OF ANY
MAMMAL –*AS MANY*
AS **32** *YOUNG AT*
EACH BIRTH

THE BUTCHER BIRD

IS SO NAMED BECAUSE IT IMPALES ITS PREY ON A THORN OR BARBED WIRE -- MUCH AS MEAT IS HUNG ON A BUTCHER'S HOOK

THE YELLOW-FOOTED MARSUPIAL MOUSE of Australia, HAS RIDGED FOOT PADS AND LONG CLAWS THAT ENABLE IT TO WALK UPSIDE DOWN AS EASILY AS *IT CAN RIGHT SIDE UP*

THE GIANT PANDA
LOOKS LIKE A BEAR, YET
THE HUGE BLACK-AND-WHITE
POPULAR ANIMAL, WEIGHING
UP TO 300 LBS., IS
CLASSIFIED BY MOST
ZOOLOGISTS AS A MEMBER
OF THE RACCOON FAMILY

THE GAR
HAS AN EXTRA SET OF TEETH
AT THE ENTRANCE TO ITS STOMACH

THE NEST OF THE RIFLE-
BIRD, OF AUSTRALIA,
TO FRIGHTEN AWAY
PREDATORS, IS ALWAYS
DECORATED WITH A
SNAKESKIN

THE **TREE KANGAROO** MAKES LONG FLYING LEAPS THROUGH THE TREES IN WHICH IT MAKES ITS HOME

THE MANATEE

which has been on earth some
50,000,000 years, is a sea mammal
related to the elephant — even having
*TOENAILS AT THE ENDS
OF ITS FLIPPERS!*

THE
FLYCATCHERS
OF PANAMA
ARE THE ONLY
SPECIES OF
BIRDS
*IN WHICH THE
FEMALES FIGHT
FOR THE FAVOR
OF THE MALE*

THE **BLACK-TAILED JACKRABBIT** WHICH REACHES A LENGTH OF 21 INCHES *HAS EARS 7 INCHES LONG*

THE **EAGLE** SACRED BIRD
OF THE ROMAN LEGIONS,
WAS BELIEVED TO HAVE
THE POWER TO CREATE
LIGHTNING AND THUNDER

THE FISHING MONKEYS OF BORNEO
KRA MONKEYS, SO CALLED BECAUSE OF THE SOUND OF THEIR CRY,
WADE THROUGH THE SHALLOW EDGES OF THE SEA *FISHING FOR CRABS*

RATS

MUST CONTINUOUSLY
CHEW TO KEEP THEIR
FRONT TEETH WORN
DOWN. IF THEY LOSE
A TOP ONE, THE BOTTOM
TOOTH WILL GROW
UNCHECKED AND
EVENTUALLY TEAR
INTO THE BRAIN —
CAUSING DEATH!

THE **TEETH**
OF THE TIGER SHARK
LIE FLAT AGAINST ITS
GUMS WHEN ITS MOUTH IS
CLOSED BUT WHEN THE
SHARK OPENS ITS JAWS
THE TEETH SPRING ERECT

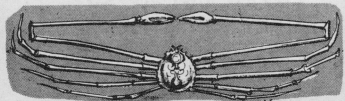

GIANT SPIDER CRABS of Japan, HAVE CLAWS 12½ FEET LONG

THE **PARADISE FISH**
OF THAILAND,
BUILDS ITS NEST
UNDERWATER,
BRINGING AIR FROM
THE SURFACE, AND
SALIVA TO CREATE
*A NEST OF
BUBBLES*

THE AFRICAN CATFISH
TO FIND ITS FOOD
LEAVES THE WATER
EACH NIGHT AND
CRAWLS ON LAND

WHITE TIGERS ARE FOUND NOWHERE IN THE WORLD
EXCEPT REWA PROVINCE, INDIA

THE GIANT PIED-BILLED GREBE

is an expert swimmer and diver, but it cannot fly, can hardly walk and is found only on Lake Atitlán in Guatemala — where only some 200 still survive.

THE ERMINE

IS SO FASTIDIOUSLY CLEAN THAT HUNTERS IN ARMENIA CAN CAPTURE IT BY ERECTING A LOW MUD WALL AROUND IT OVER WHICH IT WON'T CLIMB FOR FEAR OF GETTING DIRTY

THE **GREAT** **ANTEATER** of South America HAS NO TEETH--IT CRUSHES ITS FOOD WITH SPECIAL MUSCLES IN ITS *STOMACH*

THE MONGOOSE

IS NOT IMMUNE TO A COBRA'S BITE ʷYET IT CAN SWALLOW A COBRA'S HEAD AND POISON GLANDS WITHOUT ILL EFFECTS

THE GALÁPAGOS ISLANDS TORTOISE CANNOT BE IDENTIFIED AS MALE OR FEMALE UNTIL IT IS AT LEAST FIFTEEN YEARS OLD

THE **OKAPI** of Africa, CAN WASH ITS OWN EARS WITH ITS 11-INCH TONGUE

THE **SEA SNAKE** AFTER EATING A FISH WITH SPINES EJECTS THE SPINES THROUGH ITS BODY WALLS

The LARGEST AND STRONGEST ANIMALS ON EARTH ARE **VEGETARIANS!**
ELEPHANT, GORILLA, HIPPOPOTAMUS, GIRAFFE, RHINO, WATER-BUFFALO, MUSK-OX, ETC.

THE DIPPER
A SMALL THRUSH-LIKE BIRD OF NO. AMERICA, WALKS UNDER-WATER

THE **DEEPEST SWIMMER IN THE SEA**
BASSOGIGAS, A FISH
CAUGHT AT A DEPTH OF
23,400 FEET

A COYOTE
CAN SENSE THE PRESENCE
OF WATER BENEATH THE
EARTH AND WILL LOCATE
IT BY DIGGING THROUGH
*TWO OR THREE FEET
OF TOPSOIL*

THE BOWHEAD WHALE
HAS A MOUTH ONE-THIRD AS LARGE AS ITS ENTIRE BODY

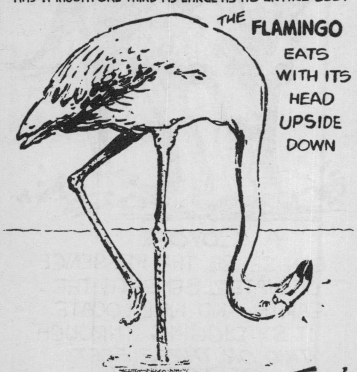

THE FLAMINGO
EATS
WITH ITS
HEAD
UPSIDE
DOWN

THE AMAZING PILOT PORPOISE
OF HATTERAS INLET

"HATTERAS JACK" a white porpoise FOR A PERIOD OF 20 YEARS GUIDED EVERY SHIP IN AND OUT OF HATTERAS INLET, OFF THE COAST OF NORTH CAROLINA-- AND *NEVER LOST A SINGLE VESSEL!* IT WOULD SWIM AROUND EACH SHIP TO GAUGE ITS SIZE AND DRAW, WAIT UNTIL THE TIDE HAD REACHED THE PROPER LEVEL, THEN LEAD THE VESSEL SAFELY PAST THE TREACHEROUS SHOALS AND REEFS-

"HATTERAS JACK" FIRST APPEARED IN 1790 AND DISAPPEARED IN 1810 WHEN THE PLACING OF BUOYS AND BELLS MADE HIS ASSISTANCE UNNECESSARY

THE **SITATUNGA** African Antelope *SLEEPS UNDER WATER!*

THE SEA LIONS on Seal Rocks, San Francisco, Ca, *ARE LEGAL RESIDENTS OF THE CITY*

THE **SQUIRREL** USES ITS TAIL AS A SUNSHADE, AN UMBRELLA AND A BLANKET

THE MEXICAN HUMMING BIRD

BUILDS A TINY NEST THE SIZE OF HALF AN EGG SHELL -- USING SPIDER WEBS AND PLANT FIBERS -- *THEN* *CAMOUFLAGES IT WITH MOSS*

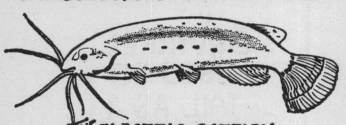

THE ELECTRIC CATFISH

SHOCKS SMALLER FISH TO DEATH -*ONLY TO EAT THE FOOD THEY HAVE SWALLOWED BUT NOT YET DIGESTED*

CARIBOU
ARE THE
ONLY TYPE
OF DEER IN
WHICH **BOTH**
THE MALE
AND FEMALE
HAVE ANTLERS

THE FAMILY OF BATS INCLUDES SOME 900 DIFFERENT SPECIES

EVERY YEAR, THE ARCTIC TERN TRAVELS A ROUND-TRIP DISTANCE OF 22,000 MILES- FROM THE ARCTIC OCEAN TO THE SOUTH ATLANTIC!

A NEW-BORN
KANGAROO
CAN HIDE BEHIND
A POSTAGE STAMP
-IT IS ONLY
ONE INCH HIGH

THE GIANT SQUID
HAS EYES THE SIZE OF A BASKETBALL

HIC

BIRDS
AND OTHER ANIMALS AND
INSECTS, BY EATING OR
DRINKING PLANT MATER-
IALS THAT HAVE FER-
MENTED, CAN BECOME
INTOXICATED

THE
SICKLEBILL
HAS A
TONGUE
SO MUCH
SHORTER
THAN ITS
BILL, THAT
TO EAT, IT
MUST TOSS
ITS FOOD
HIGH IN
THE AIR
SO IT WILL
DROP INTO
ITS MOUTH

A SMALL BOTTLE OF SEA WATER
CONTAINS 5 MILLION MICROSCOPIC PLANTS AND ANIMALS

THE DRAGON FISH
THE COELACANTH
A FISH WITH A HEAD
LIKE A DRAGON OF
MYTHOLOGY··· UNTIL ONE
WAS CAUGHT IN THE
INDIAN OCEAN IN 1938
*HAD BEEN THOUGHT EXTINCT
FOR 50 MILLION YEARS*

PENGUINS

dive deeper into the ocean
for food than any other
nonmarine animal, according
to researchers of the
Scripps Institution of
Oceanography and the
British Antarctic Survey,
—often descending
more than *785 FEET*

THE
WANDERING
ALBATROSS
WITH A
WINGSPAN OF
UP TO 14 FEET, HAS THE
*LONGEST WINGSPAN OF
ANY LIVING BIRD*

THE HEDGEHOG

EATS DEADLY POISONOUS TOADS
WITH NO ILL EFFECT, THEN FROTHS
AT THE MOUTH AND LICKS THE
RESULTING TOAD TOXINS ONTO
ITS SPINE TO PROTECT ITSELF
AGAINST PREDATORS

THE
LONG-EARED BAT
OF EUROPE
AND AFRICA
HAS HEARING
SO ACUTE IT
CAN DETECT
A MOTH IN
FLIGHT

THE *SWIFT*
THE FASTEST OF ALL SMALL BIRDS, *CAN FLY 170 M.P.H.*

THE AARDVARK
of Africa, to fully
utilize its sharp
claws, always fights
LYING ON ITS BACK!

THE **AEPYORNIS** of Madagascar
A BIRD WHICH
BECAME EXTINCT ONLY
IN RECENT TIMES, GREW
TO A HEIGHT OF 10
FEET, WEIGHED 1,000
POUNDS AND LAID
AN EGG SO LARGE
THAT ITS SHELL
HAD A CAPACITY
OF 2 GALLONS

THOSE "TALKING" FELINES
CATS CAN UTTER
9 CONSONANTS
AND 5 VOWEL SOUNDS

THE HYRAX of Africa
IS ONLY THE SIZE OF A RABBIT
-- YET IT IS RELATED TO
THE RHINOCEROS

THE **NEST** OF A BALD EAGLE *OFTEN WEIGHS 2 TONS*

A **CHEETAH** CAN ACCELERATE FROM ZERO TO 45 MILES PER HOUR IN *2 SECONDS*

THE **SACRED COMB** A FISH FOUND ONLY IN LAKE TIBERIAS, ISRAEL, *HATCHES HER EGGS IN HER MOUTH* THE FEMALE, CARRYING THE EGGS IN HER MOUTH UNTIL THEY HATCH, CANNOT EAT DURING THE HATCHING PERIOD

EVERYTHING GROWS ON AN ELEPHANT BUT ITS EYES!

THE **TRUNK** OF AN ELEPHANT HAS *40,000 MUSCLES*

*T*HE **GREAT BLUE HERON** CATCHES FISH BY *SPEARING THEM WITH ITS BILL*

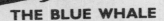

THE BLUE WHALE

which can reach 100 feet in length, makes a whistling sound so loud that it reaches 188 decibels, the loudest of any living creature — *SURPASSING THE 170 DECIBELS OF A JET PLANE!*

THE **STRANGEST OPEN SESAME** IN NATURE

THE HERRING GULL HAS A BLACK MARK ON ITS BEAK AND ITS YOUNG CAN INDUCE THEIR MOTHER TO REGURGITATE A FISH AS THEIR FOOD ONLY *BY TAPPING THAT SPOT*

A BROWN BEAR

(Ursus arctos)
of Alaska, at some 900 pounds
the world's largest
land-dwelling carnivore, during
the summer catches up to 40
salmon a day and gains 300
pounds just from its fish diet —
*BUT SHEDS ALL THAT
WEIGHT DURING ITS
WINTER HIBERNATION*

ELEPHANTS
ACCORDING TO CORNELL
UNIV. RESEARCHERS,
COMMUNICATE WITH ONE
ANOTHER OVER LONG AND
SHORT DISTANCES BY A
"SECRET" LANGUAGE OF
LOW FREQUENCY
SOUNDS BELIEVED
TO BE CAUSED BY A
FLUTTERING SPOT ON
THEIR FOREHEAD

**FRESH-WATER
CATFISH**
IN THE TROPICS
*CAN CLIMB
A HIGH WALL*

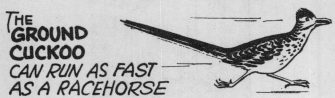

THE GROUND CUCKOO *CAN RUN AS FAST AS A RACEHORSE*

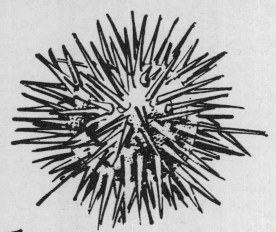

THE **RED SEA URCHIN** CAN DRILL CIRCULAR HOLES IN *ROCK, CONCRETE AND EVEN IN STEEL PILINGS*

THE
**WORLD'S
RAREST
ANIMAL**
THE TAKIN,
PART GOAT, PART COW, PART
BOAR AND PART ANTELOPE,
IS FOUND ONLY IN THE
MOUNTAINS OF TIBET, AND
*THERE ARE FEWER THAN
100 IN EXISTENCE*

THE **ELEPHANT** IS THE ONLY ANIMAL THAT HAS *FOUR* KNEES

AN OCTOPUS

that weighs 70 pounds,
because it has no backbone
can squeeze through an opening
as small as an old silver dollar

THE DECORATOR BIRD
THE MALE SATIN BOWER BIRD
ACTUALLY PAINTS THE WALLS OF ITS
BOWER NEST--*USING A FIBER BRUSH
DIPPED IN CHARCOAL AND SALIVA*

THE TINY PUDU DEER
OF COLOMBIA AND
SOUTHERN CHILE
WEIGHS 15 POUNDS
AND IS ONLY
12 INCHES HIGH

TROUT

HAVE SUCH REMARKABLE VISION **THEY CAN FOCUS SIMULTANEOUSLY ON BOTH NEAR AND FAR OBJECTS.** THEIR HEARING IS SO ACUTE THEY CAN PICK UP SOUNDS 20FT. AWAY AND CAN DETECT EVEN A TINY WATER FLEA

THE **SPIDER MONKEY**
HAS NO THUMBS
BUT IT CAN CARRY
FOOD TO ITS MOUTH
*WITH THE FLEXIBLE
END OF ITS TAIL*

THE BLUE WHALE
HAS SUCH LARGE BLOOD
VESSELS THAT A FULL-
SIZED TROUT COULD
EASILY SWIM THROUGH
ITS VEINS AND ARTERIES!

THE **WOLF FISH**
WHICH GROWS TO
A LENGTH OF
7 FEET
HAS SO VICIOUS
A BITE THAT
ITS TEETH
*LEAVE MARKS
ON AN IRON
ANCHOR*

THE **CHANTING GOSHAWK**
OF SOUTH AFRICA
IS THE ONLY BIRD
OF PREY *THAT SINGS*

SNAILS

COME IN ABOUT 18,000 SPECIES...
SNAILS OF THE DESERT SLEEP FOR UP
TO 4 YEARS...THE SNAIL'S MOUTH,
NO LARGER THAN THE HEAD OF A
PIN, HAS SOME 25,600 TEETH

THE **GIANT BLUE MARLIN**
TO EXPEL FOREIGN OBJECTS, CAN EJECT ITS STOMACH OUTSIDE ITS MOUTH, INSIDE OUT, *AND THEN SWALLOW IT AGAIN --*

THE ANTEATER

DARTS OUT ITS TONGUE
160 TIMES PER MINUTE
AND EATS UP TO
30,000 ANTS
A DAY

I GOTTA GO
ON A DIET!

THE HIPPOPOTAMUS

HAS A STOMACH
OVER 10 FT. LONG.
IT CAN HOLD MORE
THAN 400 POUNDS
OF FOOD

VISIT THESE RIPLEY'S MUSEUMS

Ripley's Believe It or Not! Museum
7850 Beach Blvd.
Buena Park, California 90620
(714) 522-7932

Ripley's Believe It or Not! Museum
175 Jefferson Street
San Francisco, California 94133
(415) 771-6188

Ripley Memorial Museum/Church of One Tree
492 Sonoma Avenue
Santa Rosa, California 95401
(707) 576-5233

Ripley's Believe It or Not! Museum
19 San Marco Avenue
St. Augustine, Florida 32084
(904) 824-1606

Ripley's Believe It or Not! Museum
202 East Fremont Street
Las Vegas, Nevada 89101
(702) 385-4011

Ripley's Believe It or Not! Museum
202 S.W. Bay Blvd.
Mariner Square
Newport, Oregon 97365
(503) 265-2206

Ripley's Believe It or Not! Museum
901 North Ocean Blvd.
Myrtle Beach, South Carolina 29578
(803) 448-2331

Ripley's Believe It or Not! Museum
800 Parkway
Gatlinburg, Tennesse 37738
(615) 436-5096

Ripley's Believe It or Not! Museum
301 Alamo Plaza (across from the Alamo)
San Antonio, Texas 78205
(512) 224-9299

Ripley's Believe It or Not! Museum
601 East Safari Parkway
Grand Prairie, Texas 75050
(214) 263-2391

Ripley's Believe It or Not! Museum
115 Broadway
Wisconsin Dells, Wisconsin 53965
(608) 254-2184

Ripley's Believe It or Not! Museum
P.O. Box B1
Raptis Plaza, Cavill Mall
Surfer's Paradise, Queensland
Australia 4217
(61) 7-592-0040

Ripley's Believe It or Not! Museum
Units 5 and 6
Ocean Boulevard, South Promenade
Blackpool, Lancashire
England

Ripley's Believe It or Not! Museum
Yong-In Farmland
310, Jeonda-Ri, Pogok-Myon
Yongin-Gun, Kyonggi-do, Korea

Ripley's Believe It or Not! Museum
Aunque Ud. No Lo Crea de Ripley
Londres No. 4
Col. Juarez
C.P. 06600 Mexico, D.F.

Ripley's Believe It or Not! Museum
4960 Clifton Hill
Niagara Falls, Ontario, L2G 3N4
(416) 356-2238

Ripley's Believe It or Not! Museum
Cranberry Village
Cavendish, P.E.I. C0A 1N0
Canada
(902) 963-3444